W9-BAA-476

Contents

the declarations

earth

The Pantyhose Declarations

The Pantyhose Declarations

poems by Nan Lundeen

Cover photo by Ron DeKett.
Grateful acknowledgment is made to the following where some
of these poems first appeared in print or online: *Illuminations,
Horizons, The Petigru Review, Iowa Writes, Happiness Holding
Tank, South Carolina Poetry Initiative.*

Digital conversion and jacket design by John Adam Wickliffe.

Copyright 2009 by Nan Lundeen.

For my sisters with love, mirth, and reverence.

goddesses

the declarations

Do I Have to Wear Pantyhose?

They look down their noses and ask if I will
sit on the committee,
make a presentation,
take a job with the corporation.

And I want to know—
do I have to wear pantyhose?

They ask if I will teach a class,
speak to the congregation,
accept a most officious task,
and sit on yet another committee.

And I want to know—
do I have to wear pantyhose?

They ask if I will host the symposium,
teach the workshop,
sing for disadvantaged tots,
and sit on yet another committee.

And I want to know—
do I have to wear pantyhose?

They ask if I will witness the execution,
provide them with locution,
marry the candlestick maker in the finest clothes,
listen while the many unburden their woes.

And I want to know—
do I have to wear pantyhose?

Oh, give me your bare legged,
your grandmother in tennis shoes,
your gardener in old boots
your hikers
your wanderers
your dreamers
the barefooted—
grass and chicken shit
between their toes—
but do not,
oh, do not
give me pantyhose!

Accepts Criticism Well

they say we must–

the parents, the teachers,
the supervisors, the minister
in her pulpit like a sassy squirrel,
ass upended on a tree trunk
scolding a trespasser–

all those connoisseurs of proper
who reproach us for our own good
while we swallow, believe and wind up
reruns and reruns and reruns of

that bulbous, icky, prickly,
conniving, insistent, deafening
whisper behind our minds

!you're not good enough!

therefore,
we must
accept criticism well.

Life after Lutheranism

In my sixties now,
I wonder how
I puttered away
my days.

Beside the stream
in my back yard
I sit in despair
crying out,
Raison!
Raison d'etre,
where are you?

Elusive bitch
I thought I had her
several times:

teaching Lutheran Sunday school
loving my children
wooing the Muse
not teaching Lutheran Sunday school
letting my children's freedom ring
wooing the Muse
searching for the path, the path
earning a damn living
battling for the public's right to know
wooing the Muse
a run at vegetarianism on the path, the path

None of it seems exceptional except—

hugs,
black sky with moon
my hound dog
rubbing her head
against mine
the scent of warm milk
in a red Iowa barn
your brown eyes.

Duty Train

I'm fifty-eight years old
and I ain't ridin' that duty train no more.

I'm stepping off and stepping down
and stepping out, yes, I am.

Let the I-should-you-should-we-should-conductor howl,
let that sneering white-haired engineer
point his long, long finger at me–

I'm fifty-eight years old
and I ain't ridin' that duty train no more.

I'm sleeping long and sleeping neat,
I'm surprising my sweet
handsome husband between the sheets,
I'm ripping off my pantyhose
and running round in my bare feet,
I'm donning my ragged denim shirt
and digging in the dirt.
I'm following the Tao of Me
dancing under the poplar tree.
I'm feeling myself up
and feeling myself down
I'm sipping from the loving cup
drumming circles all around—

because
you know it,
you better believe it,
stand back,
what I tell you is a fact—

I'm fifty-eight years old
and I ain't ridin' that duty train no more.

Crate

Robert's Dairy
Omaha, Nebraska
Misuse Punishable by Law

What's the deal here?
An old, red plastic crate
announces it will not be misused
or the misuser shall go straight to
jail.

Maybe pay a fine, I think.

What is misuse of a red, plastic crate?

Does jurisprudence have
an opinion on red plastic crates?
What is the crate canon?

Let us apply reason:
the crate was meant only for milk
and other use constitutes misuse.

Now I'm worried and confused—
what about cream and cottage cheese?
My God, what about yogurt?
Does feta step over the line?

I strongly suspect
my scribbled poems
smudged on the backs of napkins
are violations.
That sets me to worrying
about the crate police.
Will they knock on my door
in the middle of the night armed with a warrant?

Do they have a right to search?
What constitutes probable cause?
I suspect being a poet
is cause enough.

But surely this is paranoia
and what counts
is that I have always been
kind to the crate
although once I made it carry a cactus.

Wicked Wednesdays

She barges into her office
wheezing like Vesuvius with bronchitis,
grabs the photograph of her cute kids and the cute dog
in front of the Christmas tree,
heaves her nameplate down a polished hall
where it skitters like her heart in its cage,

and slams out the door forever.
The other secretaries cluck about the *poor girl*
with emotional problems, failing to see
a woman bursting with undeclared Wednesdays.

She could have vented on Wednesdays, you know,
in brief, poisonous spurts—
served him coffee with too many sugars,
phoned the wife instead of the mistress,
punctuated incorrectly,
stapled too forcefully—

What if we declare Wednesdays not nice days?

The thing is
you start not being nice on Wednesdays,
pretty soon it bleeds over into Thursday,
just the morning, mind you,
but the following week it might seep into the afternoon.

And after that?

Maybe it scuttles backward into Tuesday.
On an early Tuesday evening, you let checking
your son's homework slide
while you soak in a tub and read a mystery.

Just little things like that.

Maybe Tuesday morning you hear yourself
telling your boss, no, you won't meet his deadline,
yes, it can be done, but you're not going to do it.

And on Monday you order yourself
a whole package of really
smooth, pricey ballpoint pens and then, of course, there's only
Friday and Saturday and Sunday ...

The Redemptive Red Bra

upon the occasion of my 62nd Valentine's Day

mirror, mirror, on the wall
my pair of girls used to stand so tall
but overnight I'm shocked to see
dear Goddess, however can this be—

mirror, mirror, on the wall
what's this dangling? oh, my God, the fall!
oh, for the day we still looked young
but no more, no more, the bell has rung

mirror, mirror, on the wall
we have a eureka! —take us to the mall!
even at this late date
there must be a way to cheat on fate

mirror, mirror, on the wall
we hear the uplifting Maidenform call
on a rack hangs a little redemptive red bra
and the girls cheer — hurrah! hurrah!

earth

Summer Solstice

On this the longest day of the year
I pilgrimage to the banks of the Pacolet,
my North Carolina Ganges,
and find a tuft of grass—
spears laden with sun and seed
nodding on a block of rock
while the relentless mountain river gulps round.
These brave roots anchor in sweet moss
on the brink of the untamed.

Strawberry Daze

I wanted you
in the strawberry patch.

Our young bare knees
bore the black imprint
of Michigan river bottomland;
our baskets brimmed
with yellow-speckled strawberries.

Home to your rental house
on Maple Street
where the cat came and went
and you never tried to keep her.

Already waiting for me in bed,
you laughed
while I vamped
in a black slinky slip.

We made love
hot and solid,
devoured
thick whole-wheat
bread,
our chins slick with strawberry jam.

I wanted you today
in the strawberry patch.

Our knees
bear the red imprint
of South Carolina clay;
we pluck extraordinarily warm berries
under June sun.

They dangle in clumps
as if gathering strength
for parting
in the fullness of time.

You wear your
green brimmed hat,
the one you bought
for our trip to the Grand Canyon;
you pull weeds as you go,
a childhood habit
even though this isn't our patch of ground;
I love you because
you are a caregiver of Earth;
brown-eyed husband,
fifty now,
and still that laugh
and still those
translucent red jars
gather on our kitchen counter.

If I Could Be

anywhere at all
I would be outside
to see how
monarchs migrate
and frog skin breathes,
how birds' feet shape
to grip trees, shrubs, or weeds,
how milkweed seeds fly
and what kind of cactus turtles munch.
I'd see how spiders hinge trapdoors
and how many rooms a chipmunk bores,
how a big, bumbling bear
suddenly adept, snatches lunch,
how a spider lives beneath the sea
in her very own bubble home.
I'd discover all that
and wonder why a cricket chirps.
Does he chirp to cheer the hearth
or for some other reason?

The Acrobatic Mathematician

From a distant branch
while whisking his bushy tail,
he whips out his protractor,
squints, takes aim,
considers geometric values
and lets fly.
Undeterred by embarrassing tumbles,
finally, he succeeds!
He has calculated correctly,
has careened off the baffle accurately;
he hugs the mesh, tail twitching
and curls around the sunflower seed feeder.
Today, a full belly.

falling into night

Saluda, North Carolina

day wanes
slowly in Saluda
sunlight sifts air
feathers whisper
under pale lit sky
hammock becalmed
swims butterflies

river over rock
river over rock

there

light fades

tin roof glinting
trilling chameleon tail
now you see it
now you don't

river over rock
river over rock

woods full under half moon
sliced cleaver straight
like gram cut her pumpkin pie
this world

the other world
glimpsed like fairy feet
moon cool dips frog pond
whippoorwill song
light falling into tomorrow

river over rock
river over rock

they read the tarot
that afternoon
at Betsy's kitchen table
two friends

listen

hear that

baby birds
those are baby birds

river over rock
river over rock

white half moon
pale in the gloaming

wings flapping
owl over road
swooping low

river over rock
river over rock

cottage side yard
meadowlike
cupped in woods

there

it falls

the dark

and the lawn
fills with fireflies
fat bright fireflies

blink

blink

blink
and over there

more

river over rock
river over rock

moon bright now against black

owl
moon
alone

but for the black bear
napping in day lilies

river over rock
river over rock
river over rock
river over rock

Bliss

In summer winding green
creek banks
unaware
of the fall to come,
tumble lovely into dark
murmuring as they go.

Swollen-bellied this morning with rain
the creek
has delivered her burden downstream,
leaving a trickle
to ripple
under the dragonfly's wing.

Gathered at the rim
poplars pulse
slow as their roots probe
Gaia for water
in the pockets
of her rich summer robe.

Their mortal leaves flirt
with last light
but the old, stoic trunks
hide their faces
from the coming night.

The chickadee shifts on a branch,
mutters
into sleep;
hidden insects prowl the Earth
singing their unknown songs
each to each
steady, steady, steady
like a
heart
beat.

Victory Garden

Bedraggled August garden
shrieks orange and fire red
into hot skies
like an old, old woman
eyes defiant
refusing to take her bath.

Life in a Pot

The leek, white and fragrant
spiral slim slicked rings
fall apart, float.
Life in a pot.

The green bean, pristine and simple
conjures childhood gardens,
Gram's slim fingers pluck.
Life in a pot.

The carrot, deep and mysterious
hairy orange root crop
planted in the dark of the moon.
Life in a pot.

The squash, yellow and whole
strong and dependable,
firm gold fills the palm.
Life in a pot.

The broth bubbles and sweats,
aroma-swollen
lid gently chatters.
Life in a pot.

What You Can See in November Woods

The praying tree
one gray arm curved upward

as if she were
a war veteran

who refuses to relinquish faith
is clearly seen

now that fall
has spent her leaves.

Dawn in December

at dawn
the trees appear
in the wood
one by one

they have endured
the night
and each morning
I am surprised
to see them

a large tree
thick of trunk
and many-limbed
seizing the sky
upon the hill
appears like a specter
then takes shape
in morning light
like an old soul
reborn

December Sun

Not light-hearted like
the sun of spring,
not tender and nostalgic
like the sun of autumn,
not fraught with passion
like summer's sun
who carries a bit of recklessness
in his pocket,

December sun gleams subdued
in his beauty
hanging low in southeast sky
at ten a.m.,
rays dropping like tears
on red berries blooming by the brook.

Walking with the Dog In Winter

From the rise
Joy and I
can see the woods behind our house.

The top branches
point bare fingers at the sky.

The morning sun takes them,
and they meet the light
like sea fans catching a wave.

Companion

In memory of Missy Dog

My little dog
keeps me company
while I brush my teeth.
Nobody else I know
will do that.

Winter Solstice

as Earth
winds inexorably
down,
curls into herself
black-bedded
star and moon
cradled,
ever the mimic
I yearn for internal
communion,
hearken to womb
whispers,
mine treasures—
mirth
trust
hope
sequestered
within
the unafraid dark soul.

April at Pearson's Falls

Spring is as if
the Earth is born anew
already old.

The purple trillium
lifts its praying petals
to leaden skies;

the rumbling Pacolet
roars over slate
forcing a narrow gorge;

and the trees—the trees,
broken limbs dangling,
joints askew with age

the trees—the narrow trees
seemingly dead
everywhere singing with frothy green.

goddesses

Mathilda Lundeen

The wintergreen she rubbed into her knee
mingled
with roses.

I still see her
at age eighty, picking up her skirts
and wading through the creek
to search out
shy ferns hidden in the bluffs.

Or gathering the eggs
scratching chicken dirt with her fingernail,
Bosh, a little manure can't hurt you.

She argued with her children
stalked upstairs, blue eyes
ablaze,
insisted on molasses in the rye.

Her mother died
when she was eight
and Gram saw her
one night on the stairs.

In her rocking chair, stitching
quilt blocks,
That was Judith's party dress
and that Aunt Clara's apron,
she wove
long stories
about Cynthia's cow, goblins, and British generals—

Snuggled close in bed
we whispered late at night
about romance, boyfriends.
I don't trust that one.
Eyes too close together.

She was right.

An Assault Against Prudence

Tart against blue sky
cherries quiver
when she plunges
her ladder high
climbing past her daughter's
alarm,
Ma! get down, you'll break your arm.
Leading the assault
against birds and prudence, Gram
presses on.
Determined those black birds will
not have pie,
she pitches cherries
pinging into a pail.
On the back porch
Gram's fingers nimble
and callous from thimbles
and needles
tweak the pits
until they pop
from faded red shells,
wounded pulp
to be jammed into jars.

The Women in our Family Wore Corsets

Aunt Geneva damp from her bath
tosses more powder
into the breach,
yanks, shifts, pulls,
dances from leg to leg
like a sumo wrestler
fighting with that damn corset
on her wedding day.

Gram poses on the sidewalk
at Geneva and Alvin's farm
head high, twinkle in her eye.
I know
her proud bearing
is staved up by a corset
under her flowered dress
and in one brassiere cup
she has stuffed a balled up sock.
I know because I sit on her bed
cross-legged
and watch her dress
fascinated by the
flap of skin that used to be her breast
watching me like the deformed lid of a lazy eye.

If Gram and Geneva knew I told you this
they would be mortified.

A Lick and a Promise

in memory of my grandmother

Tillie flicked
the paring knife in cold water
to peel potatoes and nip their eyes at the kitchen sink,
kneaded the Swedish rye and
wielded her broom with a fury every morning
to give that kitchen floor *a lick and a promise.*

She stitched blue bibbed aprons
on the treadle-Singer sewing machine from feed sacks –
feed sacks that had been stashed with mash
we poured into feeders on the straw-covered chicken house floor.
When we gathered eggs
she taught me to grab
one sinewy leg to jerk
the setters off their nests
without getting pecked.
She knew which hens were mean
and which weren't.
I used to stare them in the eye
trying to decipher the difference.
The gentle ones you just tucked a hand under
to steal their eggs,
their bellies so soft and warm
you could believe they had laid creation.

Every spring, seed packets rustling, we shook
radish and peas into straight rows of soft black Earth
and set in onions at the dark of the moon.
We planted beans, beets, carrots, potatoes, watermelon,
and always her favorite flower—
blue bachelor buttons.
She liked blue flowers
and called me periwinkle
because I have blue eyes.
Bits of stubborn soil
outlined her short nails
and crept into the creases of her knuckles.

On Decoration Day
she ruthlessly snapped stems and leaves,
stood back to critically eye bridal wreath and peonies
she arranged in Mason jars
for the graves of our dead,
among them her grandbaby twins
buried over there in Illinois
in a cemetery we always had trouble finding.

She mixed and squished
bread, milk and congealed gravy
in a chipped enamel pan
her mittened hands faithfully carried to the barn cats
through the snowy Iowa dusk.

Deftly she drew houses and fences and barns–in color–like magic
on my chalkboard while we sat on the sofa
listening to 'Sky King' on the floor-model Philco.

Precisely she cut out quilt patches in her
rocking chair upstairs beside her bedroom window
where she could keep an eye on the garden;
she made me a star quilt;
she thought that was appropriate.

Every morning
her nimble fingers
gathered the long strands of her fine hair
to wind into a bun
she fastened with pins
from her delicate hairpin jar,
the only memento of her mother.
Kjerstin had kept the jar safe
on the boat from Sweden
and the long wagon ride to the Midwest
where she survived only a few years.
Tillie hid an Indianhead penny
wrapped in a note that said
the year I was born
in the bottom of the bachelor-button decorated jar for luck.

Tillie lived to be eighty-two
but to me it seemed
just a lick and a promise,
then she was gone.

Soap Angel

We woke to an ice-colored world
that Easter morning on the farm;
I kept secret
what happened the night before.

Easter fell in late March that year,
the weather unsettled like
a restless cow about to calve,
land licked clean by heady winds.

Easter Eve the lights flickered out early;
we lit a kerosene lantern
and huddled at the kitchen table
in its puddle of light–
Mother, Daddy, and me–
over cups of rose, blue, and yellow eggs;
all around us the black house
and the thrashing storm.

One by one
we balanced the eggs on spoons
to lift them from their colors
into Easter Eve
and set them carefully
on Mother's wire cooling racks
for the Easter bunny
who mustn't have too much work,
(we helped him every year.)

Once again,
we had triumphed over weather,
as farmers do, and they sent me to the basement
for one more lantern
to light our way to bed.

Surefooted at age six,
I'd find my way
downstairs in the dark;
my fuzzy slippers
stepped silently;
I could feel
webs and whisperings
through the open steps
behind my ankles;
when I was halfway down,
a light emanated from somewhere
the other side of the furnace.

I turned around,
tried the switch at the top,
nope—
I held my breath and crept on down.

Clinging to the chimney
I peered around the old gas stove.
There, at the enameled table
a figure stood.
Her folded gossamer wings
stuck out through a bibbed apron,
the one with bachelor buttons
Gram loved;
she was stirring soap
in Gram's round pan.

I miss the fresh, clean smell, she said.
We don't need soap on the other side.

I just came down for a lantern, I said.

I sidled past her to the shelves.
My knees were shaking and
I felt as cold as I had standing
in the spitting rain
when they'd lowered her coffin
at Pine Grove Cemetery
on a lonesome November afternoon.

I took a deep breath and asked,
What's heaven like?

She hummed *Listen to the Nightingale*
and stared straight ahead,
stirring the gold, thickening soap
with the biggest wooden stick
I'd ever seen her use.
Freckles danced
on her transparent hands. I longed for her to stroke my hair again
like she used to at bedtime while she told me stories.

Easter morning,
our big elm in the side yard
creaked, encased in glass, limbs slumping
under their glittering burden.
My child's swing hung stiff
from a frozen limb
like Cinderella's slipper
forever hoping for a princely thaw.

We woke to an ice-colored world
that Easter morning on the farm;
I kept secret
what happened the night before.

Aunt Ada's Ample Ass and the Year the Mississippi Flooded

Too bad Uncle Benny wasn't around
the year the Mississippi unquelled

by sandbags, levies, and walls
teeming with rain and rats and hell's balls

rose into his back yard.
Uncle Benny and his tired heart

were long gone by then
down that other, darker river.

Aunt Ada was left all alone
on Lark Street in Clinton, Iowa

with her thinning hair and her recipes
and her pension from the lumber company.

Aunt Ada filled sandbags night after night
down there on the levy

against the river's relentless rise
into North Clinton and her own back yard.

Uncle Benny had been a card—
hair the color of a sandbar

grip like a vice, smile like a lynx
slap on the back! *Hi! Howareya?*

I was six when Ma and Pa and me
walked in their front door for a visit.

Want a piece of Aunt Ada's apple pie?
Home-made, fresh-baked.

Sincere smile, sweet ole guy.
The grown-ups shifted from foot to foot

while I pondered the offer.
I didn't quite trust Uncle Benny,

but my mouth had begun to water.
M-mm, Aunt Ada's apple pie.

Now, Aunt Ada, you understand
had eaten plenty of pie—

apple or otherwise.
But Uncle Benny was short and skinny

like a river rat.
That day I nibbled at his bait—

Yes, sir, I replied, *I'll have some pie.*
Ah! Ha! he clapped his thigh,

We ain't got any!
Like I said, he was dead

by the time the river rose
so high even Aunt Ada

shoveled sand on the levy
in the rain all aching night long.

People came from all around;
they shoveled and they bagged

and still the Mississippi rose
relentless into back yards.

On Lark Street in North Clinton
Aunt Ada tacked a screen

over the toilet seat.
Never seen anything like it—

the river, the mud, the rats—
the horror stories—

coffins drifting down side streets;
rats appearing in toilet bowls.

Poor Aunt Ada in the middle
of those long, moonless nights

checking quick before she
snatched up the screen

and sat down to strain
with all her might—

quick, quick, no time to wipe.
Why did it have to be Aunt Ada's ample ass

vulnerable on that commode?
I wanted it to be Uncle Benny

sitting there on a moonless night
benignly unaware, while the Mississippi grows

and a river rat's grin gloats
inches from his sweet behind.

He could offer that friendly fellow
a piece of apple pie.

Mother's Day

Mother, all these years
I have feared your
disapproval
your voice—
Nancy, you know better than that!
The child in me
motherless
unable to trust you
until finally
when you are eighty-seven
and we are saying goodbye again
in the nursing home,
I kneel beside your chair
and lay my head
on your breast
and cry,
cry for all the years
I tried to go on
without you
and because I am little
and sad.
You stroke my head,
My dear, dear child.

My mother,
my mother.

Welcome home.

Songbird

Mother, when you tilt your head
and sing
the old lady in a chair
next to you
in the nursing home lobby
head bowed
dozing
smiles at your song
and two girls,
five and four,
sidle over to join in
when you break into
"Sing a song of Sixpence,"
fascination in their eyes.
When you fall silent,
Sarah asks,
"Is she going to sing again?"
Oh, yes, Sarah,
she will sing and sing and sing
until breath leaves her body
and carries on its wings
her Goddess spirit home.

She of Many Names

She is called Quan Yin,
She is called Tara,
She is called Mary,

Hers are the believing arms wrapped around a raped teenager
Hers is the cool night blessing a disturbed mind
Hers is the *today no* of the father who turns down a beer

Hers is the mercy of the last breath
Hers is the forgiveness in a lover's heart
She births the hope in every soul.

We are She.
We are One.
Glory be.

Quan Yin

Philodendron leaf
pales with fall
or because he shelters
a Goddess and wants
to become one with her
on these frail gray days
when we sink
toward darkness
and only an inner light beams
from Quan Yin's face
upon my altar.

The white Goddess tilts
her head listening
(I like to think
she listens for my poems)
as she has listened to human
cries throughout millennia
ever steady font of mercy,
hand poised in blessing,
sea shell birthing compassion
for our wan souls.

If I were a philodendron leaf
shading Quan Yin
I would pale, too,
wanting to be like her
and would listen
for her voice
soft as a bell offshore,
soft as a white petal
dusting cheek of Muse:
Make me a parasol of moonbeams,
weave them with hope.
You are not alone.

The Day White Buffalo Calf Came to Memorial Hospital

White Buffalo Calf blocks
her doorway,
head and shoulders in her room,
rump end, tail swishing in the corridor.

No ill will
shall enter here
protected by the intentioned tail.

The child's hospital room
fills with White Buffalo;
they crowd in
like women at a Sak's sale.

White Buffalo Calf leans a shaggy head
toward the girl on the hospital bed,
breathes through holy nostrils
into her ear.

White Buffalo breath
carries old secrets
of wise people who respect
the oneness,
the healing inherent in the holy animal spirit.

Grown to ten,
the child tall and tan
blond hair blowing in Grandmother breeze
legs hugging White Buffalo.

She Bear

with gratitude to Marija Gimbutas

In a vision
she comes, tender paws
enfold me,
dense fur
warms me to the bone
a lap
familiar like home,
curve of crescent moon
our rocking chair,
stars our sisters.

The vision
burrows into my heart
and years later,
I find a picture –

"Goddess holding a baby,
both wearing bear masks"
Kosovska Mitrovica, Yugoslavia
Vinca culture 5300-3500 B.C.

Centuries ago women knew you,
Mother Ursa.
Help me remember
to trust you now
and when my body falls away.

Dear Persephone,

With gratitude to Charlene Spretnak

About your decision to abandon your mother–
warm growing Earth –
to carry compassion to the darkness,
did you hunch inside yourself
like a turtle scrunching deeper and deeper into her shell or did you
explore some shadowed path
alone
surrendering yourself to invisible hands.
Were you afraid?
Did you hurt to leave
brown-eyed susans, iris and wheat?
Did you think you would miss
wood ducks and brambles?
What about the brown cow lowing in the meadow
under wisp of cloud?
Did you count on coming back?
Or not?

How the souls must have savored
the sight of your purple robes
in that lonely place
when you blessed them with pomegranate.

Then there was the tug again, wasn't there?
And you decided to straddle the worlds
maybe promising to return
maybe not, maybe leaving them to meager faith.
And oh how our hearts rise upon your return
carrying a pomegranate promise
when purple-headed crocus push through snow
that somehow, somehow, it will all be all right.

Womanweave

for Diane

We carry our confusion on cushions
to each other, pluck threads,
tuck this here,
does that one go there, do you think?

We weave lives we struggle to comprehend,
of a cardinal –
your late father loved those birds –
who appeared outside

your mother's window as she lay dying;
of a mystery – a friend who turned away
when my daughter and I became victims
to something unspeakable;

of frustration – when you wanted
to protect your grandchildren
from danger but dared not
step across your family's line in the sand;

over the millionth cup of tea
warmed by afghans in your Michigan living room
and by whatever animal is sharing your house –
the latest, a cat named Gus,

we weave each other's lives
to create not something we understand
but something that's good enough
for us because friendship
has created the tapestry.

November White

for Diane

Whiteness of a summer's day
flown
the white deck chairs
snowy coverlets clinging to their seats
rest
upon brown snow-encrusted leaves
such a short time ago
dancing
and green and alive
like you and
me
a pair of old deck chairs
outlasting summer meeting
again
we drink nonalcoholic
wine and are careful to avoid
gassy vegetables,
thirty-three years
of tea and talk
coneflowers and Honda Civics
of trying to solve
the mystery
of friends who deserted
we
pursue angels
on farmhouse roofs
always aware
the snow
will
fall.

What a Circle Can Do

Dedicated to my sisters

A circle cannot protect us from death
because we are mortal.
A circle cannot protect us from change
because we are creatures of Earth.
A circle cannot protect us from conflict
because we are human.

A circle can heighten our awareness
of something more—
a circle can remind us
we are more than bones and belly and skin.
A circle can remind us
there is something sacred.

We see it in each others' eyes;
we feel it in the love that flows among us.

When we are awed
by the spiral dance of life,
the awful mystery,
a circle is our place to reach out
and find a sister's hand.

7601206R0

Made in the USA
Charleston, SC
22 March 2011